MW00934721

This book is dedicated to my wife Brittney and son JC. You've taught me more about leadership than anything or anyone else in my life.

It's also dedicated to the hard-working people managers that are striving to make their teams happy and successful. And to the organizations working to support those managers.

4 ENGAGEMENT VS ACCOUNTABLE

Table of Contents

Introduction

LEADERSHIP IS
ALWAYS ABOUT
PEOPLE.

SIMON SINEK

I've been fascinated by the topics of leadership, management and teamwork for as long as I can remember. I've practiced these things for years in a variety of settings, studied it in a master's degree program from a great school, and have done a lot of individual research and there's a lot of great stuff out there and some not and I believe still more to come.

What makes a great people manager? Put simply: a lot. Like parents, there's a lot expected of us as people managers. It can be exhausting, frustrating, thankless, lonely and one of the best, most rewarding experiences of our lives. Also, like being a parent, there are common things that make great people managers great.

Superheroes are great not because of their abilities but because of their love and service to people. And the same goes for super managers.

Ray Dalio in his book *Principles*[1], says that a manager is really a process engineer. I agree with him. And I would take it a step further and say that they are also culture, team and people builders and engineers too.

The Case for People Manager Development

People manager development is one of the single greatest priorities in organizational life today. As the world gets more complex, fast and connected, organizations need their people to think and act creatively in order not only to survive but thrive. Just look around at the number and frequency of organizations that have ceased to exist because of this very problem.

Gallup has reported for more than a decade that people are not happy in their jobs. Employee disengagement is costing U.S. employers an estimated half of a trillion dollars. That's right, trillion with a "T".

Both Gallup and Google, through their surveys and studies, have found that an employee's relationship with their direct manager has the single most impact on their performance and connection and satisfaction with the company itself.

So, it's managers within companies large and small that are shutting down and stressing out their people. They are the cause of employee disengagement and they are the solution. Yet, it's not their fault.

Did you know that only 1 in 10 people have a natural ability for people management? And leadership and soft skills are the least adequately developed of any other type of skill in the workplace.

However, with technology advancements making the world a smaller place and consumers increasingly intolerant of things like poor quality and service, soft skill development is growing in necessity.

If you're are a people manager, current or aspiring, then I would say develop yourself. Depending on the degree of development from your company, you may need to take all the initiative yourself, but you and the people you lead will be better for it.

Maybe your company has some training that's voluntary or ad hoc. Take it all. If your organization doesn't have any training, do it yourself. Chapter 11 is all about self-development so you can get more direction and guidance there.

For those of you who are organizational leaders, I implore you to develop your people managers. Make it an organizational priority to build systems and a culture of leadership development. Chapter 12 covers this in more detail.

What's Your Ideal Boss?

I would like you to try something. Think to yourself of the best manager you've ever work for.

Now think of the qualities that made them great. Go ahead and list them in your head or on paper if you'd like.

Next think of the worst boss you've ever worked for (statistically, nearly all of us have worked for someone that we did not enjoy reporting to for at least some if not all of our professional lives).

Now what made them not fun to work for?

Have your two lists?

Backstory

Being Vulnerable

Like most everyone I've experienced great and poor leadership in every aspect of my life. It's either true or me being a victim, but other way, I would say poor leadership, personally and professionally, has affected me more than great leadership. That's why I'm so passionate about it now. I've spent most of my life pointing to the type of leader I didn't want to be. But pointing to what not to be isn't holistic and is more negative in nature.

In the last decade or so, I have pointed to and learned from positive leadership examples and devoured everything I can learn from and about great leadership.

I'm proud to say I've grow significantly as a leader at home and work. Yes, it has also made me a better husband and father. I still have a long way to go but bringing great leadership to the world and helping others in their leadership journeys has become my passion and mission and will ultimately lend to my own personal growth too.

Developing Other Leaders

A couple of years ago I wanted to create a leadership and management development academy for a small organization for which I was responsible. Reason being was that we had a deficit of prepared leaders to take on existing or soon to be open, management positions which didn't include the exponential and rapid growth we were anticipating. We were headed for a serious leadership crisis and potential failure in achieving our vision.

We needed a comprehensive, yet simple approach to develop the leaders with all the necessary skills, so I went back and reviewed all my work, studies, hundreds of books, tools and materials on management and leadership to find it. I couldn't find the exact thing I needed so I went back into research mode. That's when I found what I thought was the best, most accurate, thorough, comprehensive and simple description and resource that summarized the qualities of a great manager. I found Google's "Project Oxygen".

Project Oxygen

Everybody knows Google. Mostly for the searching of information on the internet of course. Like Kleenex, the company has become synonymous with the product and has become the verb and noun to describe it. Not only is Google a wildly successful product and service company, it's a great company to work with and within. The founders, Larry Page and Sergey Brin, would tell you it's the culture and the people that enabled the success. To this today, Google is a coveted, sought after employer with a repeated award-winning company culture.

Back in 2002, still in its early years, Google tried something crazy, which isn't so crazy for a progressive company breaking molds. They eliminated managers. The reason they tried this is because they figured they had really bright intelligent people working for them who didn't need to be "managed". Managing was oppressive and they wanted a different kind of company and culture.

Larry and Sergey quickly learned their lesson and brought managers back within months.

What did they learn? That managers really are important. But why? In 2008, once they had an even bigger team and more resources, they set out to answer that question. The charged their people operations team with a project to figure out why and to what extent managers were important and have it be rooted in data like everything else at Google.

They called it this endeavor Project Oxygen.

Because, according to Lazslo Bock in his book *Work Rules*[2], great managers are to an organization what oxygen is to us as humans; a necessity for survival.

They conducted the study for nearly 18 months and interviewed hundreds of Googlers (the name they give employees of their company) and hundreds of Google people managers. Trends started to emerge and the differences between great teams and managers versus not so great teams and managers become clearer and clearer until they had a list of 8 qualities of what made the best managers at Google the best.

Here is that list.

This list resonated with me because it was short and simple but also covers what I believe to be nearly everything a manager needs to know and do to be successful.

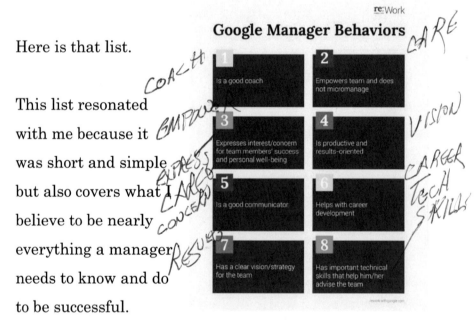

Google Manager Behaviors

re:Work

1 Is a good coach	**2** Empowers team and does not micromanage
3 Expresses interest/concern for team members' success and personal well-being	**4** Is productive and results-oriented
5 Is a good communicator	**6** Helps with career development
7 Has a clear vision/strategy for the team	**8** Has important technical skills that help him/her advise the team

Handwritten annotations: COACH, CARE, EMPOWER, VISION, EXPRESS, CAREER, TECH SKILLS, LARGO, CONCERN, RESULTS

How does Google's list stack up to the two lists you came up with? Pretty close? That's at least what I've found doing this dozens of times, no matter the group, restaurant managers, new shift supervisors, US Air Force pilots and officers. The result is always the same.

Now let's understand the implications of this. Google essentially just proved that successful teams and organizations (which hopefully all of us can agree Google is) of the modern era are led by managers that are not necessarily all-knowing, decisive, charismatic, fearless, ultra-competent, highly powerful, influential and prophetic unlike what the last several centuries have led us to believe. Instead, they serve, build and lift up their people.

Now that's a big deal.

You see, we all want a lot of the same things from our leaders.   Someone who is invested in and cares about us and inspires and motivates us.

This is where we are going. The world is demanding it. It will eventually happen and I hope everyone gets on the bus sooner rather than later.

Who is this book for?

This is the book I wish someone would have handed me when I first became a people manager.

It's for people wanting to become people managers, people about to be or just recently promoted to people managers, experienced people managers who feel they need more development to increase their impact and success. And it's for organizations of all sizes that want one resource to help create an institutional leadership development program and process.

I wanted this to be one of the most comprehensive, thorough, practical and transformative tools any individual leader or organization could use to develop great people managers and leaders. It focuses primarily on the people side of being a manager. Reason being is that once you become a people manager your business is people. Hiring, firing, culture building, community building, team building, people development, career development, communication and the list goes on. Leading people is a full-time job and requires a lot of skill that unfortunately most organizations do not properly assess or develop.

This book will not go into things more technical in nature like finance, marketing or other skills and training that you may need depending on your industry, business and specific job.

However, fortunately for you most organizations have way more emphasis and resources for technical and business training than they do people leadership training so you should be good to go.

Plus, if for some reason your organization doesn't have what you need, there are vast volumes of books, classes, etc. on more technical, "hard" skills in comparison to the "soft" skill training in this book so you wouldn't have to look far outside the organization to find training for yourself.

This book is like reading 20 books in 1. I will distill down for you some of the more important aspects of people leadership and management of the past couple decades and give you both the key learnings and practical advice to implement, improve and become the best people manager you can be.

Some other things to know

Humility

Even though it's not listed there are a couple other qualities that will be critical for you to have to go on this journey of growing as a people manager and leader.

The first is humility. Humility is not thinking less of yourself but thinking about yourself less. I know that this is pretty counter-culture to our society as a whole and the grand majority of corporate cultures, but it is in fact the single most important aspect of effective leadership.

Leadership is taking care of those around us. This is what leadership is.
-Simon Sinek

Most of the love lost from people in their institutions whether it be government of business is from leaders of those institutions acting selfishly, sacrificing others so they may gain[3].

Humility is not just essential to leadership as a whole but learning as well. If you confidently accept that you have more to learn then you'll be more open to it.

I can't reiterate enough that humility is foundational to growth, as a leader especially. Because being a leader means you are entrusted to take care of the lives of those around you, especially when you have a title and positional authority.

Because once you step into a role of formal or positional authority, it's no longer about you. It becomes about helping the people around you. Leading those in your charge to advance the mission of the organization. That's where humility comes in.

Growth

We current and aspiring people managers are imperfect. We need to give ourselves grace and space to fail, to not have all the answers, to not always have to be strong. When we do, then we can grow.

Failing is part of this process. It is not a bad thing or something to be avoided. It's where growth happens.

Bock puts it this way, "because many professionals are so good at what they do they rarely fail. So, once they do they don't learn from it. They become defensive, deflect and screen out criticism. The ability to learn shuts down at precisely the time when they need it most".

So, embrace the discomfort, the failure and floundering at times. That's how you grow. You, your team, your organization and your family all deserve the best version of you. So, keep pushing.

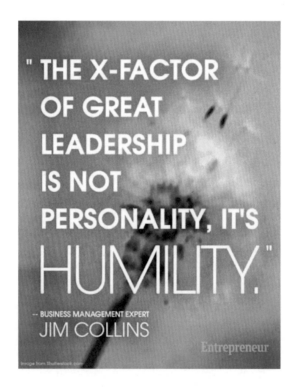

Key Points about becoming a Super Manager

1. *People managers are very important to organizational success.*

2. *People leadership skills are some of the least developed and most necessary in today's world.*

3. *The more organizations invest in their managers, they more longevity and success they will see.*

4. *If your organization doesn't have the resources to help you, commit to growing yourself as a people manager for your own and your team's sake.*

5. *Leverage Project Oxygen to give you a list of skills to focus on to grow comprehensively as a people manager.*

People Leadership Development

Personal Reflections

Chances are you've experienced great and not so great people managers. What do you feel were the differences?

What was the impact on you and the team and organization?

What would you have liked to have seen and felt differently?

Can you be that change? How?

Next Steps

Grade Yourself as a People Manager

Coach

- How am I as a coach? Do I give too much direction or allow others to test, try, fail and learn? Am I there with them to help them learn without taking over?

1- Not great   2   3   4   (5 –) I'm the master!

Empowerer

- Quick to give power over decisions to others? Trust others to get the job done? Thorough invest in other's skill and clarity of mission?

1- Not great   2   3   (4)   5 – I'm the master!

Empathizer

- Do I care about the people on my team? Do I show it well? Do they believe it?

1- Not great   2   3   (4)   5 – I'm the master!

Results Driver

- Do I get things done? Do I help my team be productive? Do I have systems in place for my own and my team's productivity?

1- Not great 2 3   (4) 5 – I'm the master!

Communicator

- Is my team well informed? Do I give them everything I know? Do I go out of my way to over-communicate? Do I build systems that enable open communication?

1- Not great 2 (3) 4 5 – I'm the master!

 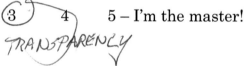
TRANSPARENCY

Career Developer

- Am I invested in my team's career's? Do I put them out front to get development and recognition? Do I match projects with skill development and career aspirations or just to get stuff off my plate?

1- Not great 2 3   (4) 5 – I'm the master!

Visionary

- Do I know the future that is right for our team? Do I passionately share that future every chance I get? Is it grounded in the organization's purpose?

1- Not great   2   3   5 – I'm the master!

Technical Competence

- Do I know enough about our business to be dangerous? Can I help out or advise enough when needed?

1- Not great   2   3   4   5 – I'm the master!

Tally Your Score

35 – 40 = Throw this book away, you don't need it!

25 – 34 = Your pretty solid but let's do some growing

16 – 24 = You got some decent room to grow, you can do it!

15 or less = You're either just starting and need to really consider whether being a people manager is right for you.

Chapter 1
Great Coach

Each person holds so much power within themselves that needs to be let out. Sometimes they just need a little nudge, a little direction, a little support, a little coaching, and the greatest things can happen.

-Pete Carroll, NFL and NCAA football coach

"Put me in coach!"

Sorry, I just always wanted to say that but was never good enough at any sports to get a chance to do it as a kid. So, I tried it out on you.

But this isn't what we mean by "coach" in our working lives.

Coaching seems to really have been popularized over the last few decades, but unfortunately it looks to have lost some of its original meaning and intention. One of the places I worked years ago, when someone used the word "coaching", most employees immediately got afraid because the word was synonymous with "getting in trouble" or "getting a talking to". It was never really a pleasant experience. I didn't really know what coaching was back then but knew it shouldn't be that.

What is Coaching Really?

Coaching is nothing more than helping others grow. It's that easy and that difficult.

Less than a quarter of coaching is effective!
-Michael Bungay Stanier

Just imagine if it was better. If it was the opposite? It would change our organizations and our lives!

So, Then What Does It Take to Coach Well?

Know Your People

What it basically means to help someone grow is that we have a trusting relationship with the people we are coaching. We have to know their strengths, their weaknesses, their goals, fears, anxieties, skills and the list goes on. So, if we want to be great people managers, we have to be great coaches, and if we want to be great coaches, we have to build caring relationships with our people.

DON'T OWN THEIR PROBLEMS!

Ken Blanchard in *One Minute Manager Meets the Monkey*[4] describes this best with his monkey analogy. If you haven't read the book, the basic premise is that problems, tasks and projects are "monkeys".

And when we as coaches and managers take our people's monkeys, then we're enabling them, robbing them of growth and development and overburdening ourselves. It's a great way to teach and better understand delegation and ownership through using the visual of a "monkey".

Ken's message is one of delegation and empowerment but the same applies to coaching. If anything, as a leader that wants to grow the skill and independence of their people and enable greater team impact, performance and productivity, delegation is a most and more about growing ability than getting stuff off our plate.

For example, once as a manger in a department that was administrative in nature I was told by the leader of a part of the department that several of his team members were asking for standing desks. I would have to get approval from my boss to make the change and it would have required a decent amount of research and planning.

I resisted the temptation to want to be the savior of my team and accomplish something for them by fulfilling their request. Instead I realized the value of having them take on this project.

If they owned it then they would have to work together as a

team, assign
roles, do the
research, do some
testing and make
a plan. More
importantly they
would have to
take personal
responsibility.

It's easy to throw out ideas, requests and problems to "management" to solve. It's an entirely different story to be truly empowered and the results, or lack thereof, to be squarely on your own shoulders, in other words, to have the full well-being of your monkey's thriving or dying squarely in your own hands. Now that's great development and growth right there!

If I had looked at this from a purely selfish standpoint I could have either easily said no or said that's not my monkey, you keep it.

Which I did, but with different intention and purpose.

Same result but different impact. Rather than the team feel unheard or sluffed off I said "great idea, how are we going to make it happen"?

And then I asked questions to get them starter and put ownership squarely back on their shoulders.

Ask Lots and Lots and Lots of Questions

As the coach at work, typically what people are doing is something related to task, function, solving a problem or taking on a project. So, you're coaching will come in the form of questions rather than overt direction.

In his book, *The Coaching Habit*[5], Michael Bungay Stanier shares some of the best coaching questions possible:

- What's on your mind?

- And what else?

- What do you want?

- How can I help?

- What was most useful?

These questions are great because they keep the responsibility and action with your coachee and they require them to think, which is perfect, because that's how we all grow.

Carrying on the standing desk project example, asking questions is how I led off with the team.

Why do want these?

How would they work?

Where will we get the money for them?

Have you test driven before we buy?

These questions did two things: forced them to think and own the project. Both grew them as individuals, employees and leaders. They didn't just get to lob the suggestion grenade my way and run. They needed to treat it instead like their precise, adorable, sweet monkey and make sure it grew up well.

Grow Them Through Questions

Some other helpful questions come from a coaching model used at Google called the Grow Model. You can see the questions here in the visual. They're similar to some of the above questions, but at least give you some different wording and approach.

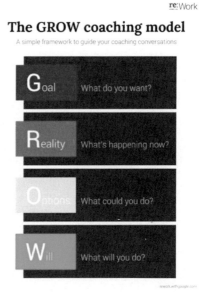

Rewording questions can be helpful at times when your coachee is stuck and doesn't know what you're asking or where you're trying to take them.

Be Right There with Them in Deep Practice

Dan Coyle discovers this thing he calls "Deep Practice" in his awesome book the *Talent Code*[6]. Basically, Deep Practice is when we focus intensely on pushing ourselves just outside our skill, ability and comfort zone and fail repeatedly and make small tweaks and adjustments to get slightly better each time.

So once your coachee has their plan, and after being clear they own it and have thought through possible solutions with the help of your questions, the next best thing you should do is be right there with them as they try it in action to help them make adjustments as needed. If for some reason you can't be right there with them, then have someone take your place, or make sure to follow up as soon and as quickly as possible to ensure the learning cycle is rapid and that reflection is always a part of the process.

Let Them Fly

Being a great coach also means we have to be secure with ourselves and seeing others succeed, potentially beyond what we ever accomplished. That can be a hard pill to swallow when we're the boss and we got there because of our skill, ability and accomplishments. But when you're a people manager, it's about them now and your success is their success and vice versa. If our personal insecurities as a people manager hold someone else back, we both are losing.

The better you are as a coach, the greater performance you will bring out of your team. So, keep practicing for your own and your people's sake.

When Not to Coach?

Coaching isn't always the answer though. I know, I know. I started with preaching how great and important coaching is. And it is for the grand majority of your performance and problem-solving conversations, but there are times not to coach too.

This diagram is one of the best I've seen at illustrating

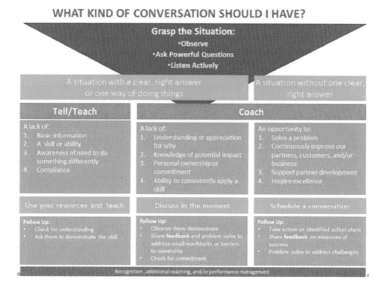

WHAT KIND OF CONVERSATION SHOULD I HAVE?

Grasp the Situation:
•Observe
•Ask Powerful Questions
•Listen Actively

A situation with a clear, right answer or one way of doing things		A situation without one clear, right answer
Tell/Teach	**Coach**	
A lack of: 1. Basic information 2. A skill or ability 3. Awareness of need to do something differently 4. Compliance	A lack of: 1. Understanding or appreciation for why 2. Knowledge of potential impact 3. Personal ownership or commitment 4. Ability to consistently apply a skill	An opportunity to: 1. Solve a problem 2. Continuously improve our partners, customers, and/or business 3. Support partner development 4. Inspire excellence
Use your resources and teach	Discuss in the moment	Schedule a conversation
Follow Up: • Check for understanding • Ask them to demonstrate the skill	Follow Up: • Observe them demonstrate • Share feedback and problem solve to address small roadblocks or barriers to ownership • Check for commitment	Follow Up: • Take action on identified action plans • Share feedback on measures of success • Problem solve to address challenges
Recognition, additional coaching, and/or performance management		

when to coach and when not to. Sometimes, when someone is brand new they just need to be taught. So, show them the ropes so at least they understand the operation, team, culture, etc.

But once they are assimilated that's when the coaching should begin.

All too often I've seen managers and trainers assess someone's lackluster performance as an opportunity for "re-training". Re-training is really just code for "I'm not that great of a coach and don't know how to help them perform better".

I have never been perfect at this but I'm getting better. And I had one boss that did not change his style or approach really at all. He would ask questions just to ask questions. And it felt more like an interrogation than a robust truth-seeking conversation to expand thinking and help solve problems and grow skills.

If you already have the answer or want a specific answer then don't ask questions. Just say what you're thinking. But, remember to be open to the idea that you may be wrong or what worked in the past won't work anymore. That is another beautiful outcome of coaching. You, as the coach, should also be learning and growing.

And if you're wondering what happened with the standing desks, they were denied. Sorry for a sad ending to the story. But hey, our team was better for it just by embracing the process!

Now go get 'em coach!

Key Points of Coaching

6. *Know Your People*

7. *Don't Own Their Problems*

8. *Ask Lots of Questions*

9. *Be Right There with Them in Deep Practice*

10. *GROW Them*

11. *Let Them Fly*

12. *Coach at the Right Times*

Coaching Development
Personal Reflections

Think about the best coaching conversation or coach you've personal experienced? Why was it great?

Revisit a recent coaching conversation that you had with someone else. What impact did it have? If you don't know, go ask them.

Next Steps
Get Feedback Partners

- These can be people on your team, peers, your boss.
  Basically, anyone that can watch and/or experience
  you coaching and give you feedback about it. At least
  one of these people should be someone that you coach
  so they can tell you what they experienced directly
  and if they grew in some way as a result of their
  conversation with you.

Get a Mentor

- This could be someone you will also use as a feedback
  partner but does not necessarily be and probably
  shouldn't be. This will be someone that you reflect
  back with after a coaching conversation to share and
  learn from your own experience in being a coach.

Watch a Great Coach

- No better way to learn and be inspired then by
  watching someone that is great at what they do
  right? Well there should be at least one great coach
  somewhere in your life, and if not, there are all kinds

of great coaches elsewhere like in sports, speaking and motivational seminars and YouTube.

Chapter 2

Empowerer

An empowered organization is one in which individuals have the knowledge, skill, desire, and opportunity to personally succeed in a way that lead to collective organizational success.

-Stephen Covey, best-selling author and personal success expert

This topic is one of my favorite topics I write and teach on. I don't exactly know why. Maybe because I appreciate feeling empowered in work and life, or because as a manager I've been rewarded the most personally and professionally when I've helped to empower others. Or maybe it's when I've created an empowering environment that enables great performance.

Either way, it's not just a big topic for me, it's a big topic in leadership, management and all of business and organizational life right now and has been for some time.

Many organizations are taking up employee engagement and empowerment as strategic initiatives to improve innovation and their employee's discretionary effort and productivity.

Why Aren't People Empowered?

Many reasons, but here are just some of the big ones:

1. Our organizations have been built to consolidate and **push power to the highest levels possible.**

2. **Technology** has become a micro manager's dream.

3. Our organizations have become **rule and policy laden** all in an attempt to reduce risk associated with employees making bad decisions.

4. People have been trained since grade school to recite, **memorize, regurgitate and execute.**

5. And we haven't made it **clear enough, provided enough of the right training or made it safe enough** for people to be empowered and make decisions or take risks.

Who Cares if People are Empowered Anyways?

What'd You Call Me...VUCA!?!
Volatile, Uncertain, Complex, Ambiguous. That's what VUCA stands for and it's the acronym being used lately to describe our world today. Fitting isn't it? That's pretty close to what I feel and see all around me all the time.

In his book *Team of Teams*[7], General Stan McCrystal, painted one of the most dramatic pictures of this type of environment in our world in recent history when he was charged with leading all of US special forces against Al Qaeda in Iraq.

He talks about how despite the fact that the US military was dominant in training, technology and resources, they were not winning the war. The reason was because of how they were operating versus how Al Qaeda was operating. McCrystal's organization was functioning like a traditional hierarchy. Information goes up to the "thinkers", they plan and consider, and then instructions and direction goes down to the "doers" to execute.

This works in a complicated world, but now we're in a complex, or VUCA, world. Complicated meaning many inputs, but mostly predictable and linear, like an assembly line. Complex has many more inputs, directions and planes, closer to what it looks like in the opening hit of a billiard table. The cue ball hitting the several others causes unknown outputs of the directions of all the other balls.

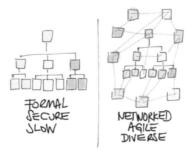

The traditional hierarchy was just too slow and cumbersome. Al Qaeda was operating so much faster because they were more organized as a loose network. Every cell operated independently, there was no "head" making all the decisions. The leader was a motivator, inspirer and communicator in this structure, guiding and nudging the entire organization in the direction of the vision and goals.

It wasn't until General McCrystal moved his organization to become a hybrid of the two structures that they started winning. The two supporting approaches he called **"Empowered Execution"** and **"Shared Consciousness"**.

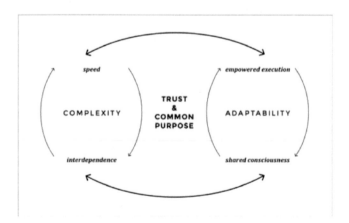

Again...Who Cares?
Great Organizations, That's Who

No one has ever achieved greatness from a place of fear or disempowerment.

If your people are scared, subtly or overtly, then you're making all the calls and taking all the risk and your team's performance is limited to you.

Organizations that have excelled in recent history have found an effective way to engage, inspire and empower their people throughout the entire organization. Patty McCord, former Chief People Officer at Netflix, even recently wrote a book about how she and the rest of the leadership team at Netflix unlocked performance through truly empowering people. The book is called *Powerful*[8] and has been one of the most recommended for 2017.

So basically, we're living in a crazy complex world and the organizations succeeding are engaging, involving and empowering every person in their organization. So now what?

Ok, If We Have to Empower, Then How?

Clarify and Unify

Simon Sinek's book, *Start With Why*[9], is the best place to start. Simon points out that we all operate from an innate purpose, cause or mission that is deeply rooted and shaped over the course of our lives. Organizations are just groups of people getting together to live out common "whys".

So, every organization must first explicitly clarify its "Why" (purpose, cause or mission) before it empowers its people. This both unifies and enables people to take 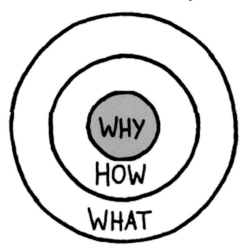 initiative and action that helps to advance the organization's "Why". As long as leaders have done a great job of bringing people into the organization that believe passionately in the same "Why" and have constantly reinforced it with them at every opportunity, then the leaders should feel confident that everyone around them will act in unity with that "Why".

Of course, people leaders should clarify the "How" and "What" as well, but only in general terms, not in hundreds and thousands and policies, procedures, do's and don'ts. "How's" are just strategies and core values and "What's" are just the physical outcomes, products, services and measures of success. But most importantly they should all be aligned with and stem from the "Why".

Train and Grow

Building skills of every kind in your team is critical. Part of what made General McCrystal and his group so successful is that his team members at every level were the most highly trained, skilled and equipped soldiers in history! This enabled him to more fully empower since he knew his teams and team members were the best trained in the world.

L. David Marquet wrote a book called *Turn the Ship Around*[10] where he tells the story of taking over the worst performing submarine in the US Navy fleet and turning into the best through empowering his team.

He points out that the two critical components that enable successful empowerment versus sheer chaos are clarity and competence.

Clarity basically has to do with the "Why" I described above and competence meaning the skill and training of the team members. Marquet worked tirelessly with his leadership team to turn their organization into a learning organization.

Every people structural change they made, they did through the lens of growing the skill, ability and knowledge of every team member. For example, he changed briefings that were passive and required no participation from the crew into drills where team members had to come prepared to describe and demonstrate their role in a future planned operation. It worked beautifully to encourage individual ownership in growing one's skills. After this change, Marquet rarely would see crew members in their living quarters playing video games and wasting time, which used to be common place. Instead he would see much more often, the crew studying, quizzing each other and supporting each other's growth.

Push the Power Down
Now it's time to give up control. That's how Marquet started his journey with his new submarine crew.

He basically stopped giving orders. What!?! I thought that's what the military is all about? It is, to a degree. And he had a lost to risk in taking this approach. A court marshal and getting thrown in jail or even people dying. It's not that he didn't take those things seriously, he just realized he couldn't do it alone.

Having a crew of 170 active, engaged, passionate thinkers was way more powerful than just him making all the decisions and taking all of the initiative. So instead he put the power in his teams' hands and he coached and guided them along. And he made sure to be constantly building up everyone's clarity of their mission and culture and skills of the entire crew.

Make Sure it's Safe

Just as importantly as clarity, competence and handing over control is making sure to be explicit about safety. I don't mean wearing hard hats or anything like that either. Of course, that's important if you work in a workplace that is physically dangerous. But what I mean here is psychological safety.

If this is new for your organization or a traditionally disempowered organization, people are going to flounder, be trigger shy, and downright fail. Make sure, to patiently, regularly, affirming say "its ok". You as the leader, have to make it safe. Make those mishaps a learning opportunity. The more you do this, the safer you make taking risks, learning and growth.

Key Points of Empowerment

1. *Empowerment matters, the world is too complex and fast to not have engaged, empowered employees making decisions.*

2. *The way to empower is clearly define and reinforce constantly the organization's "Why, How, and What", the organizational clarity.*

3. *Then give the power away. Give increasing independence and autonomy.*

4. *But as you do, make sure they are knowledgeable and competent enough to own those decisions.*

5. *And coach, encourage and make*

Empowerment Development
Personal Reflections

When was a time you felt disempowered in your job? How did that feel? How did it effect you in and outside of work?

Have you ever been empowered? What did that feel like? How did you manager empower you?

How many times to people come to you for an answer in a day? How often do you give direction versus teach to encourage independence?

Next Steps

Start Small

- Its ok just to ease into empowerment. Start by giving something away that you wouldn't normally even if its seemingly small to you.

Go Bigger

- Now give bigger things away, share more information. Empower until it hurts!

Think Like a Consultant

- It's harder to wield our power around when we have no formal authority.

Chapter 3

Empathizer

Leadership is a relationship.

-James Kouzes and Larry Pozner, creators of the leadership powerhouse franchise, *The Leadership Challenge*

Any great leader will tell you they have great love...love for their purpose, cause or mission, love for their community, love for their organizations and love for the people that entrust their lives to that leader and organization.

Care, concern and love is at the root of great leadership. If you don't love people, then please don't be a people manager. You will only make your life and the lives of others much more painful and difficult than need be.

Howard Behar's book *It's Not About the Coffee*[11] is based on the premise that people come first and he drives home the point well the Starbucks' incredible success was primarily built on this approach, coupled with great coffee as well of course.

When you love someone, you want the best for them. Like with parenting (which I'm sure you've caught on I use a lot as an example because it's universal and leadership in parenting is so much like leadership in organizational life), we want to see our kids grow to be happy, healthy, well adjusted, productive, successful contributing members of society. We want them to be good humans.

Well we have the same opportunity and responsibility with members of our teams and organizations. When we want the best for them we help them grow. Not only grow in their job and career so they can help the organization live out its "Why" better but we can also help them grow and thrive as people too.

Howard Behar has a great quote from his book that sums it up well,

grow your people and they will grow the business.

Find the Balance

The hard part about love and care and concern for you team is finding the exact right balance. On one end is over caring and on the other is caring too little.

Caring Too Little

This is at the core of what most of us have probably felt from a manager that we did not enjoy working with.

They didn't care.

If you've experienced that, I'm sorry. Whether we realize or admit it or not, it affects us. And everyone deserves to be loved and cared for, especially by those closest to us or whom we depend on. And our manager is up there with the most impactful. It's up to them, and us, as to what extent and in which direction.

Bob Chapman is a CEO of an American manufacturing company called Berry Wehmiller and he is leading the way at showing what a company led through love, care and concern for its people first and foremost can do for people, community and business. The story is incredible and I highly recommend his book, *Everybody Matters*[12].

Bob talks about a personal revelation about how he had been running his business with a traditional approach focused on money and numbers because that's what he grew up with and learned in business school. Until he started to consider the effects of the approach on the people within his business.

Mass layoffs, seeing people as titles and positions and their contribution to the personal success of business owners and leaders.

Bob rightly points out in his book that stress from work is the leading cause of heartaches which the majority happen Sunday nights and Monday mornings. He says that work is literally killing us. Or at least business as usual is. Business as not caring about people as human beings but objects for our personal and organizational success.

He started to increasingly change the way he led the company to have a more human focus. The culminating event was in the 2008 recession. His company lost a sizable percentage of business and his board insisted on layoffs to make up the difference. This is a widely accepted and used to this day approach but Bob refused.

He said it was inconsistent with their people focused culture. Instead he introduced a furlough program asking people to take upwards of a month off unpaid and told the people of Berry Wehmiller that "it would be better for all of us to give a little than anyone have to give a lot".

What Berry Wehmiller experienced thereafter was incredible. Morale sky rocketed and people started cooperating with one another to find other ways to save money and started trading furlough time with one another to take from those who could afford the unpaid time off less.

Caring Too Much

This could look like letting a personal relationship get in the way of making essential decisions for the good of the entire team of organization. Or where misguided concern could mean we take on too much of an others' emotions or problems or when we shield them from any pain or discomfort. In parenting, this is called being a "helicopter parent" and man is it hard for me not to do (as a parent more than as a manager).

When we do this, as leaders or parents, we make them unintentionally inept at thinking or solving their own problems and by solving all of their problems, we burn ourselves out and leave our team under skilled and under challenged.

Below is a visual that shows what I'm describing the empathetic range and spectrum I'm describing. On one end is apathy, or not caring much at all about the emotions and impact on others a manager can have.

On the other end is called compassion where we can physically take on the emotions of our people, exhausting both our people and ourselves.

And then empathy is ideally what we're seeking, which is not the same as sympathy or compassion. When we're empathetic as a leader we care about the emotions of others and our impact on them. Dale Carnegie puts it this way: The path to success with others is understanding their point and seeing things from their angle as well as your own[13].

How Do We Care "Just Right"?

The goal is to be an empathetic coach, mentor and consultant.

Don't Just Hear, Listen
This is called empathetic listening.

It means, take away the distractions and fully engage in completely hearing and understanding what someone is actually saying and all the things they are not saying in their tone and body language.

Marshall Goldsmith, renowned executive coach and best-selling author, says in his book *What Got You Here Won't Get You There*[14] that "people who have the skill of active listening and making others feel that they are the most important person in the room are what separates the good from the great".

This is tough. It requires real energy to do nothing but sit there and take it all in.

One suggestion before going into an important and/or potentially difficult or emotional conversation is to take some time beforehand to mediate, clear your mind and focus. Also, work to suspend judgment and just focus on listening and understanding.

Be Genuinely Curious
If you love people, then it should come natural to you to be genuinely curious about them.

Everyone's story is so unique that if you as the leader just regularly ask people lots of questions from the place of learning about and from them, I'm sure you'll be blown away. I know I am the more I learn about my team.

This is also why empathy is really one of the foundational and most important people manager skills. This is where we connect with our people and learn about their strengths, weaknesses, hobbies outside of work and the build the relationships necessary for great coaching, teamwork, career development and so much more that's required of successful people management.

Show Them You Love Them
I once told my wife that I love her so that's good enough right?

Of course not!

Say it every day!

Show it in signs of affection, doing things she likes to do and in gifts and signs of appreciation.

The same goes for the people we are responsible for. Simon Sinek points out in his book *Leaders Eat Last*[15], that we all long for a sense of belonging and that our work is valued and is part of something bigger than us. Our role as leaders is to regularly shine a light on that.

We've all heard the adage that people need to hear something 7 times before they believe it. Especially when it comes to positive versus negative reinforcement. So, say good things about and to your team all the time!

And part of learning about and building relationships with your people is learning what they love; their favorites snacks, hobbies, interests, professional aspirations, personal goals etc.

Once you learn these things, you can get them small tokens or gestures for the birthdays or work anniversaries that show you know and care about them.

Dan Coyle learned and shared in his book *Culture Code*[16] that this was a critical element of success for the San Antonio Spurs, one of the winningest basketball teams in recent NBA history.

The coach, Greg Popovich, also known as "Pop", is well-known by his team and organization as a gentle, tenacious, high standard fatherly figure.

He goes out of his way to build trusting, respectful, connected and engaging relationships with his players and everyone supporting his team.

One tradition that highlights this well is that Pop loves to have meals together with his team and coaches and every trip on the road includes meals as a team. Pop spends a lot of time choosing where to go that everyone would enjoy and hand selecting the menu and wine.

Then at the end of the season, Pop gives a scrap book to every team member with menus, wine and memorabilia from each of the restaurants they eat out at while out on the road.

Being an empathetic people manager is the key to being a super manager in every capacity as a people manager. It starts with caring, listening and learning about our people and acting based on what we learned.

When we care about our people, the rest of leadership comes very naturally.

Key Points on Empathy

1. *Care about your people*

2. *Take time to listen*

3. *Learn from what you hear*

4. *Show your people you care and know about them through praise, appreciation, gifts and challenging work and projects that use their skills and talents.*

Empathy Development
Personal Reflections

Have you ever had a boss that you felt cared about you?

How did it feel? How did you know they cared?

What do you know about the people you manage? Do you know the names of the most important people in their lives (spouses and kids)? Do you know what their passionate about?

Next Steps

Go Out of Your Way to Interact

- Have lunch in the breakroom with them, stop at their desks, work side by side with them. This will give you the opportunities for connection and learning.

Start Asking Questions

- Start asking questions of and about your people in every setting you can. Ask how their day is going, ask about their family, hobbies outside of work, how they think work is going. And things change over time so ask regularly.

Use What You Learn

- Keep a binder or some sort of record of what you learn to reference back to. Some managers give forms to fill out of interests, but you don't do this to your spouse, so why do it to your team. Learn about them naturally.

Chapter 4

Results Driver

You can't get results, you can't experience your potential, if you don't take action.

-Howard Behar, former President of Starbucks

Getting stuff done is pretty much the end goal, the point and purpose of why we have our job and what others like our teams, bosses, shareholders and customers need and expect from us as people managers.

The great news is, the better you become at all of the other people manager skills covered in this book, the better results are and the easier they come because your people are helping even more.

Driving results as a people manager is two-fold: you getting stuff done and getting stuff done with and through others.

Get Er' Done

The quote made famous by Larry the Cable Guy is a leadership and personal effectiveness mantra. If you want to be effective in life and in leadership then live it, love it, breathe it!

Being productive and results driven involves two parts: Mindset and System.

Mindset

The first thing you have to have is the right mindset. Do something. Just get after it. Don't let anything get in your way.

Once you get something in the inbox, either delete, delegate, plan or ditch. Don't let it just sit there indefinitely and don't just defer. Deferring will get you and the pile will only grow.

So, get your mind right and train yourself to have a bent towards action.

System

Once you have the right mindset and you are ready to get after it, build yourself a system to manage it. For example, I'm all electronic. Stuff into my inbox, I check it by either phone or laptop and it either gets deleted, filed, delegated, done or planned for. If I've delegated or planned for it, I both flag it in the inbox with the date I need to do it, or I book time right onto my calendar to get it done, or flag it for when I plan to check in with the person owning it.

This is just an example and by now means flawless. The point is that piles on your desk or 1000 emails in your inbox with 257 unread are not a very good or manageable system.

Some people like paper more. If so, get a planner that you like.

Delegate

Part of the system needs to be clarifying what you own and why. Realistically, it should be pretty little. That doesn't mean you are going to be bored. On the contrary, your role is people manager, team leader and culture champion. Those are full time roles. If you are too busy with tasks then who is doing those other critical roles?

That's right, no one.

So, do not, do not, do not, fill up you plate with stuff. Your system should involve the stuff going directly to or between your team.

Not delegating is vicious and cyclical and neither you or your team will ever be fully and lasting in success. This visual illustrates this concept well, along with the one in the chapter on coaching.

I am also constantly evaluating what I should be owning and what others should be owning. The less I directly own, the more flexibility I have to ebb, flow, help others and exercise all of the other people manager skills to enable success of my team.

And by the way,

when you get things done and follow up on commitments you make to your team, you build trust, confidence and culture.

Pacesetting the Team

The more important part of your role as a people manager is to help your team get things done, to perform. Once you have a system to enable and free up your own time then you can get busy helping your team with theirs.

Help Them Get Organized

This means doing the same for individuals on your team the way you did for yourself. Help them prioritize and set systems for themselves. And its ok if it's a different system or style then your own.

The litmus test for a great organizational system is how long it takes to get things done.

If your team member is spending inordinate amounts looking for things. No go.

Or if they can't even find what they need to get their job done. Nope, not organized.

Focus on the process and result of the process but your team member will be more likely to follow through on a system if it's their own design.

Build Team Systems

This is the ultimate team results machine. The best performing teams are focused on collective results and each member is clear and accountable on their part in contributing to the success of the team. I'm going to talk more about teams and what makes great ones in Chapter 9 but here I'll introduce an organizational, results-oriented tool that helps the entire team.

This can be as simple as in your weekly team meetings when problem solving or idea sharing on how to get closer to attaining your team goals, ask the idea sharers to own their idea to fruition and report back to the team each meeting.

It's similar to your individual organization system in that there's prioritization, flagging, planning, delegation and follow up, but way more powerful! The reason it's more powerful is because you will be doing all of these things together as a team. So, you can talk about who wants to take on what, what steps should be taken, etc.

Plus, the natural and healthy peer pressure that comes from knowing the entire team will be checking in the following week is invaluable. Everyone knows that each person will responsible for reporting back to the team whether or not they followed through on what they owned.

Team Scorecard

The team scoreboard is the tool that helps in the above described process. The tool comes from the Table Group and can be read about in a few of their books including Organizational Health[17] and Politics, Silos and Turf Wars[18].

I've personally used this tool for several years now in several different settings, teams and industries and it really is universal. It serves multiple purposes. It's a place to capture the organization and/or team's "Why, How and What" (more on these in Chapter's 7 on vision and 10 on culture). Basically, these are the mission, strategic anchors and the Thematic Goal of the team. Below is an example.

The Thematic Goal helps in rallying the team toward a common focus. This goal is the team's most important near-term priority in helping to advance the organization's overarching cause or mission.

The boxes below the thematic goal are the Defining

Goals

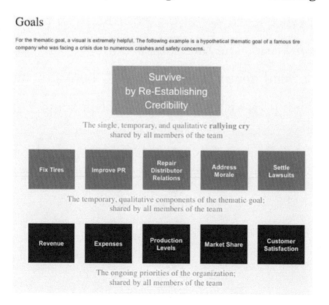

For the thematic goal, a visual is extremely helpful. The following example is a hypothetical thematic goal of a famous tire company who was facing a crisis due to numerous crashes and safety concerns.

Survive-
by Re-Establishing
Credibility

The single, temporary, and qualitative rallying cry shared by all members of the team

| Fix Tires | Improve PR | Repair Distributor Relations | Address Morale | Settle Lawsuits |

The temporary, qualitative components of the thematic goal; shared by all members of the team

| Revenue | Expenses | Production Levels | Market Share | Customer Satisfaction |

The ongoing priorities of the organization; shared by all members of the team

Objectives that define (thus the name) in more detail the Thematic Goal. Below that are the Standard Operating Objectives which are basically the everyday priorities that the team must also monitor that are not explicitly covered in the Defining Objectives.

The driving results part of your role of people manager with and through the team come in as you use the tool. Below is an actual example of one of my own scorecard I used with one of my own teams (hopefully I disguised well enough what organization I was with at the time).

So, what happens is in the weekly team meeting (more on meetings in Chapter 9) the team scores themselves on all of the Defining and Standard Operating Objectives. This is basically setting the priorities for the team that week thus focusing everyone on the team's efforts towards furthering the thematic goal in some specific way.

Next, you as the facilitator ask the team what should be prioritized and how exactly to get after those priorities. It may take some coaxing on your part but ideally what should happen is people with the right strengths are volunteering for tasks or functions as a part of the planning process for that week or better yet being encouraged and volunteered by their peers. Then you are someone on the team captures these commitments and send them out to everyone so all are clear as to what needs to be done and by whom.

Then you as leader can be checking in on progress and encouraging others to do the same. But don't worry too much about pushing along in haste. Allow for the next step to unfold.

Next when everyone comes back again the following week, have everyone share back on progress on their commitments. That way they are accountable to the team and not necessarily just "the boss".

In using this process, I was blown away at the team building that came as a result. And I was ultimately thrilled with the things we achieved in an incredibly speedy amount of time with far less stress on my part and everyone's by adopting this simple process.

No matter what the measure of our success as a people manager is the results we achieve with and through our teams. The measure of a great manager is if they can achieve great results by inspiring, nurturing and growing their people.

Results without caring are just empty results.

-Howard Behar

Key Points of Results Driver

1. *Build a results mindset in you and your team*

2. *Develop your own organizational system that ensure information and task effectiveness with minimal effort from you*

3. *Only have things on you plate you should be doing like people managing, culture and team building*

4. *Help your team develop their own organizational systems*

5. *Embrace team organizational systems*

Results Driving Development
Personal Reflections

Do you feel like you have plenty of time to get your job done? Does your team?

Is your team getting the results you would like? Do you know why and how so it can be repeated?

Next Steps

Start with Action Orientation

- When something comes in the inbox deal with it in some way. Start small and just get after it.

Evaluate the Systems

- Step back and review your own personal organization system. Do you think it's working? Maybe give it some tweaks or an overall if necessary. There are lots of great tools out there. If you think yours is great, teach it to your team to help them and see if it does.

Team Systems

- Now look at systems of how you team interact and help each other with work, planning and prioritizing. I highly recommend using the one I suggested but there are others out there too. Just remember to focus on getting the team to be as accountable to each other as possible.

Chapter 5

Communicator

Silence guarantees nothing will change.

-Alan Eustace, former Google executive

No one has ever complained about being too much "in the know". Have you ever heard of anyone quitting a job because they were "way to well informed"? Or has anyone ever complained about having too much transparency in their company and being too involved. Not that I've ever heard.

But I've definitely experienced a lot of the opposite. "No one knows what's going on around here", "no one tells me anything", "I'm always in the dark". Sound familiar? I thought so.

Communication is vital for any organization's success. People have to know where they're going, why and all the necessary daily information to allow them to do their jobs.

You Talky as the Leader

Yep, if you're a manager, you're going to have to talk. Honestly, the style doesn't matter as long as it informs, inspires, challenges, motivates and lifts up your people. You really are the gatekeeper of information on your team. It's up to you if you want to be a funnel or a water fall.

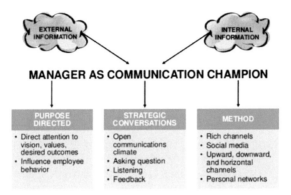

Individual

The first level of communication you'll have to do is one-on-one with individuals. You'll need to be articulate, clear, understandable and relatable. First this requires something seemingly contradictory, what I mentioned in Chapter 3...empathetic listening. That's right. In order to be a better communicator, we first have to listen. Listening helps us to understand our audience better so we then know how to best connect.

And then before delivering a message think of the point or purpose. Doing this will ground you if you get questions, concerns or pushback. Because then you can redirect back to the point and purpose of the message.

For example, if its constructive feedback you're giving then you can share with you team member that you care about them and the team but what they're doing right now is not great performance and is ultimately holding everyone back. It may sound harsh but wouldn't you want to know? I was floored to recently read that 2/3 of managers are uncomfortable communicating with employees!

No wonder so many people feel uninformed. And if we don't, who will!

We have to commit ourselves as people managers to communicate with our team members no matter how uncomfortable, challenging or time consuming it might seem. If your intent is to help, serve and care for your team they'll realize it and will respond accordingly.

Group

I don't know this for sure but I'm willing to venture to say that public speaking is one of the most common fears out there. Unfortunately, you as the manager don't get that luxury. You're going to need to address at the least the people you lead in a group setting, probably pretty often.

Thankfully it's very similar to individual communication in a lot of ways. First there's understanding your audience, knowing what drives them, inspires them and their needs. Once you know those things, you can better tailor a message to touch on those needs but while sharing something you may need too as well.

In order to do that well, planning and preparation is even more vital for group communication since the nerves will most likely be in overdrive. Take the time to bullet point out your key thoughts/themes.

And then belt it out with confidence. I did some acting in high school and college and little did I realize how much it would help me in communicating confidently to a group of people. Lean on any experiences you had like that to build your skill and confidence in public speaking.

Build A Communication Ecosystem

You can't be the only talker. You need to build a team of talkers (not just gabbers and jabbers) in order to have a well-informed team and organization.

Platforms

Email, phone calls, team meetings, huddles, communication boards, newsletters, Facebook, GroupMe. Do all of those and you're good.

Drop mic.

Kidding of course. I hear a lot of leaders ask, which of these is best? And the answer is all of them all the time! Use them all, just for different things at different times for different people and groups. And get your team to decide what works best for them. If they have a say in deciding what tools to use and how, then they're more likely to embrace and actually use them.

Information Channel	Information Richness
Face-to-face conversation	High
Videoconferencing	High
Telephone conversation	High
E-mails	Medium
Handheld devices	Medium
Blogs	Medium
Written letters and memos	Medium
Formal written documents	Low
Spreadsheets	Low

And then most likely you will have to do a lot of the heavy lifting at first to use the platforms, especially the newer ones until more people start adopting.

I started a Facebook group with the last organization I led and you'd think with a mostly younger crowd they would jump right on it, but that wasn't the case. They had to realize that it was safe and valuable and after I and our leadership team starting posting, it soon took hold and helped to dramatically improve direct communication across the entire organization and made it feel much smaller.

Habits

This is the most important part. What most people don't realize is that they can make themselves and others more informed on their own! Unless you are a micro-managing, control freak of a manger, I imagine you don't care if Sally shares with Bob that the latest process in another part of the team or organization is changing. Why have it go through you?

The more you push your team to share information and communication more broadly then the more it will just become second nature.

I just finished reading a book called *The Power of Habit* by Charles Duhigg[19]. In the book, Paul shared a story about the power of an organization, Alcoa, that started focusing on safety habits and it ended up transforming every other aspect of the company, including and especially communication and information. This in turn transformed performance in all other areas of the company just simply by focusing on the communication habits of the everyone within company.

Key Points of Communication

1. *The most effective communication is face to face. You as the manager are the chief communicator so you should be doing it a lot.*

2. *Listening is the first step in effective communication.*

3. *Talking as a group is also very important for connection, problem solving and efficient information sharing.*

4. *You as the manager should also be creating and leveraging all communication mediums at your disposal to build a communication ecosystem where team members help each other stayed informed.*

Communication Development

Personal Reflections

Have you ever been a part of a team or organization that you felt did communicate well? How did that feel?

How about a team that did communicate well? How did that feel?

Do you spend most of your time of the day communicating?

What would your ideal communication ecosystem look like?

Next Steps

Assess Communication

- Start with your own. Ask for feedback about how well you communicate.
- Then ask around about general sense for communication within the team.

Evaluate the System

- Find out how people on your team currently get information.
- Consider the effective of those tools and either go more in with them, replace or eliminate the ineffective tools.

Practice Communication Often

- There are all kinds of ways to grow in personal and group communication skills.
- Read, study, listen, practice and feedback, mentors, speaking clubs

Chapter 6

Career Developer

You can never stop being a teacher. It is the core responsibility of a leader.

— Alex Malley, **TV personality**

As people managers and leaders, we have the awesome opportunity and responsibility to help people grow.

Obviously since our capacity of being a people manager relates mostly and specifically to work that then becomes the growth we talk about first. But when we hit on the right development of ourselves and those we lead, it should absolutely impact us personally too. The better I've become as a leader at work, the better husband, father, sibling, friend and community member I've become too.

This is the opportunity we have. To have real impact on people's lives by helping them become the best versions of themselves in every part of their lives. Oh, and did I mention that as they perform better at work consequently your team as a whole will perform better.

Find the "Why" and Then the "What"

Many of us have a very specific definition of what career success looks like. Typically, it's associated with title and money. I know it has been for me. Only very recently have I started to reevaluate and evolve that definition to be more about using my strengths to positively impact others.

Ultimately it doesn't matter how we define success. All that matters is that we people managers can help others define their success and help them move closer to their goal.

Find "Why"

What I've done with anyone I have ever coached or mentored in their career journey has been to start with the question, "why"? Why are you here at this company? Why do you want that promotion? Why do you do what you do?

Many of us don't know and that's typically what we need to do first. Answer why we want that promotion? Is it because you love growing and developing people or because you think that that is just the natural progression of things or you want more money? If the strengths of your people and their innate drives and motivations are not aligned with the career trajectory that they think they want, then they will be very unhappy. Even if they're making more and have higher status and prestige.

The heaviest, most emotional and critical part of helping someone in their career path is first helping them learn their "why".

Then the "What"

Once the "why" is clear, the "what" becomes the strategy and plan. Having the "why" be clear can help to identify what kinds of things your mentee needs in order to grow.

Once the "why" is a little clearer you and your mentee can take a look at different projects and functions, inside and even outside your team, to see what would makes sense for them to take on.

You could even strategically look at things with multiple wins that for example simultaneously help them grow and take something off your plate or move a project forward.

And of course, don't forgot to have them write it down and plan time for regular check ins. This helps to make sure things stay in track and that your mentee is getting the right balance of challenge and mastery and is progressing towards their goal.

Culture as the Ultimate Development

Everyone knows that culture eats strategy for breakfast. But why? Mostly because the collective attitudes and behaviors of the people within a given organization dictates how people feel and how things get done...or don't.

If those collective norms are focused on performance and development, they can be so much more powerful than even your own direct intervention and mentorship with any one individual on your team.

Empowerment

I've mentioned Dave Marquet before, specifically in Chapter 2 of on empowerment.

One of my favorite phrases from Marquet is because of the way he ran his ship,

> *there was no need for a leadership development program. The way they ran the ship WAS the program.*

What he means is that members of the organization were regularly given stretch assignments and decision-making power to follow them through. That in and of itself grew people regularly and consistently and even fed off of itself, like a snowball or flywheel effect.

So empowering people isn't just good for innovation and getting things done. It will also be one of the single greatest drivers of personal and professional development for absolutely everyone in the organization.

Teamwork

Teamwork could go hand in hand with culture and it may not. It depends on the "why", core values and strategy of your organization. Either way, teamwork can and absolutely should be pursued if you want to provide every opportunity for growth possible to you team.

You see because when a team is really cohesive that means they are being vulnerable and transparent to one another and are so invested in each other that they would never withhold feedback from one another.

Because they care so much about each other and the team's success they won't allow any single member to hold themselves or the team back in any way. If someone on a highly cohesive team is struggling, the rest of the team doesn't hesitate to dive in and help them, which in turn improves their skill and performance along with the rest of the team.

Besides, managers only have one perspective and can potentially be out of tune, off base or just prioritizing something different. It is peers on a team that know exactly how everyone else is performing and ultimately are the best source of developmental feedback.

Key Points on Career Development

1. *Start with "why". This is the intrinsic motivator and knowing it will help you help your team members know the best route to take.*

2. *Only after the "why" is clearer, start to help your mentee with their plan of development.*

3. *The plan should include technical skill but should absolutely be enough of a stretch in other areas that they feel it in their personal lives too.*

4. *And if you want to grow the scale and impact of development beyond your own time and resources, work to build a culture of development by encouraging feedback and training amongst team members.*

Career Development

Personal Reflections

When have you felt the most supportively stretched in your work life? Did it also effect you personally for the better? How was your manager involved if at all?

Who have you helped to grow in their career? How? How could you do more of it that balances your and the team's workload too?

Next Steps

Hold "Why" Sessions

- Either 1 on 1 or as a group.
- Ask questions that go deeper into motivations, for example:
    - what do you do outside of work
    - when do you feel "in the zone"
    - what fills you up,
    - what are you naturally good at
- Help your mentee(s) draw out themes and word those things into strengths and values, or "whys"

Align "Whats" with "Whys"

- Now, with your mentee taking the lead, look around your team and other teams to see projects, roles and functions that fit with their "why" and will challenge their skills in the direction they want to go.
- For example, if someone wants to get promoted to manager because they love people and love motivating people towards a common vision then give them a project that allows them to practice

people manager skills like coaching, empowering and giving tough feedback.

- Then watch and give feedback to them and coach them along.

Nurture a Development Culture

- Foster true teamwork (more in Chapter 9)
- Encourage peers to train and give feedback to one another.
- Hold a feedback session where team members can practice giving each other feedback if they're not already comfortable doing so.
- Arrange the work area in so much a way that encourages interaction, discussion, brainstorming, etc.

Chapter 7

Visionary and

Strategist

OUR MISSION

PRETTY MUCH WHATEVER
OUR COMPETITION DOES,
BUT SIX MONTHS LATER

©marketoonist.com

Missions should give meaning. They should be moral versus just a business goal. The most powerful movements in history had moral motivations.

-Laszlo Bock, former SVP of People Operations at Google

I've already mentioned it several times now that a huge part of our jobs as people managers is to inspire our people. And what better way to do that than to paint a picture of a future that is better than today. That is essentially what setting vision is and we as leaders have the great privilege of being the facilitators of its creation, evolution and thriving.

There are lots of definition of "vision". The common themes from the best definitions involve the **future** and **a path**.

Where are we going? How are we going to get there? And why are we doing this and/or why will it matter?

Where? How? And Why?

These are the 3 vital questions any organization must answer and ensure that every individual organization member understands, believes in and acts against.

Where, How, Why

Start With Why

This phrase has become incredibly popular since Simon Sinek's book and Ted talk with the same name. For those who don't know what it means, basically it means focusing on deeper beliefs and motivations that drive our fulfillment and happiness in life. Every person and every organization have a "Why", although many haven't made it explicit and

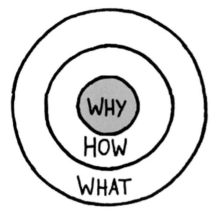

written it down. The danger in not making it explicit is that we can become misaligned with our core purpose and start doing things for the wrong reasons which can lead to burnout, failure and unhappiness.

One of the single best things we can do as leaders is to make the "Why", or purpose, cause, or mission, clear and concise and invite others aligned with it to join us. This will lead to happy people, making real impact and ultimately lead to long term organizational success.

Then Where

Once an organization's "Why" is clear, it can then paint a picture of the world it envisions. This can and absolutely should involve the measures of success too.

However, this should not only be about money or productivity.

It should include those things but should also have other things like customer and employee happiness. For example, Berry Wehmiller, an American manufacturing company, measures the divorce rate of its employees.

What!?! Why!?!

Because they figure if the company is doing a great job creating meaningful and fulfilling work and valuing their employees then they'll go home happy and treat their spouses better ultimately leading to happier marriages and families. Pretty powerful, right?

Finally, How

This is where we come up with the stuff most organizations already know to do and have framed on the walls in their hallways, which are values and strategies. The key difference here being leaders that successfully use these to drive culture and results are dead serious about them and ensure that all values and strategies are deeply rooted in and connected to the "Why" and the "Where".

Not only that, but the leader must be so obsessed with personally living out the company values and expecting everyone else around them to do the same.

I love this quote by Kevin Cushman that illustrates this. He said that...

most companies do not lack purpose or values, they lack the courage, clarity, and commitment to actually live them.[20]

Unfortunately, too many companies don't obsess about values enough to actually engrain them into everyone's minds in order to have them influence their behavior. Just like one company, as an example, that had integrity as a value. I'm sure they had frames of eagles flying through blue skies with the word "Integrity" at the bottom with a catchy phrase below that was proudly hung in every hallway of their headquarters.

Who is this company I'm referring to? Enron.

The Team as Your Partners

It can be very powerful for someone to have influence over the direction of their team or organization especially if they're not that high up in the org chart.

By involving your team in the conversation and clarification of the "Where, How and Why" you will exponentially increase their buy-in and the likelihood of success of bringing those things to life.

John Mackey, former co-CEO of Whole Foods, talks about a process like this in the book he co-authored called *Conscious Capitalism*[21]. He describes pulling together dozens of team members from across all different parts of the company and reviews it purpose, vision and strategy every few years. Mackey points to this as one of the most powerful and centering things they do as an organization which has led to much of its success as a company.

Key Points of Visionary and Strategist

1. *Every great people manager must paint a picture of a future that is brighter than today. A great vision has 3 parts: Why, Where and How.*

2. *Why*

   a. *Every organization and person must be clear on why the exist, what their purpose, cause or mission is.*

   b. *The "Why" is intrinsic and ever alive, driving us. It can never really ever be fully "achieved".*

3. *Where*

   a. *Then the vision simply becomes the future or advancement of the cause, or the natural next step in bringing the "Why" closer to reality.*

4. *How*

   a. *"How" is the strategy and plan to accomplish the vision. But it also includes the behaviors, or values, everyone in the organization must espouse if the "Why" is to be achieved and achieved the right way.*

Vision Development
Personal Reflections

What gets you inspired? Have you ever been inspired by a company or organization? Or a mission statement? Or a leader? How? How did it feel?

How could you better articulate the vision for your team? How could you build in reminders, artifacts and rituals that support and uplift it?

Next Steps

Think Hard

- Us busy people managers don't always build time into our schedules to think, but you have to give yourself some to paint the picture in your head of what you want for your team if you haven't already.

Involve the Team

- Then BEFORE you share your vision with the team ask them, both individually and as a group, what they want for the team.
- Only then should you share yours and try to marry the two.

Write It Down and Check In

- Next, plaster it all over the walls, build in some systems and routines and habits that support and remind everyone where you are going together.
- And then make sure to come together regularly and check progress towards your vision.

Chapter 8

Technical

Competence

Basically, to lead without a title is to derive your power within the organization not from your position but from your competence, effectiveness, relationships, excellence, innovation and ethics.

-Robin S. Sharma, writer and motivational speaker

At first, it surprised me when I saw technical competence at the bottom of the list of the ranking of important skills of a manager at Google. Especially because it's Google, that's kind of what they do. The other reason it surprised me is because I thought that the leader had to be the smartest, toughest, most charismatic, best trained and highest performing to be successful. And many organizations believe the same (or at least act that way by promoting that way).

So, to see people skills ranked above technical competence was surprising. However, the longer that I've been a people manager the more I understand why.

But it is important to point out that it is still absolutely on the list. Effective leadership and management is not either technical or people competence, but both.

Know Enough to Be Dangerous

Several years into being a people manager I learned from other managers that leading was different from doing and so the pendulum swung hard the other direction and little emphasis was placed on technical skill.

But that wasn't right either. Now I believe the answer is somewhere in the middle.

In order to be effective in any of the other people manager skills covered in the earlier parts of this series you will have to have at least a base level understanding of the functions of your team. Especially in order to coach and drive results. And it builds trust by jumping in with your team when there're swamped or need to accomplish something important. But be careful not to go to far and take over and disempower them or become a crutch and get stuck with an overflowing plate.

Knowing enough, technically speaking, can also help you help your team make process and system improvements. They may be so used to something so dysfunctional or not valuable that if you learn what the end result is and how to use the tools and bring your own perspective you can potentially save them a lot of time and headache.

Culture as Competency

The more people know, the more stuff gets done right?

Consolidating competence to just management is actually limiting for a team. The best way to empower and get more done is to grow everyone's skill level.

I've referenced to Dave Marquet's story multiple times now in this series because it's so comprehensive of everything leadership needs to be today and for the future.

The core of his story is about empowerment and building a culture of greatness through a different type of leadership.

Marquet points out that there are two pillars that support truly effective empowering leadership:

Competence and *Clarity.*

Think about it. When are the times and what are the things that you don't give power and authority to others to make decisions about?

Typically, things you don't believe they have the skill in or don't understand "the big picture" about, right?

Well great news, both are totally fixable! All you have to do is inspire an environment of constant learning
and regularly share and reinforce the vision, strategy and values of the organization.

Easy right?

Well, not so much. It's simple, yes, but requires even more for leaders than does a micromanagement approach. But the payoff is so much greater.

How would your team look and feel if every single member was pushing themselves and each other to learn and grow to help everyone and the organization succeed? Amazing, right?

So, make learning the norm and freely give away knowledge and opportunities to learn and let your people blow you away.

Key Points of Technical Competence

1. *Know enough to be dangerous*

2. *Competence should be more collective and organizational then individual*

3. *Use culture as your competence builder*

Competence Development
Personal Reflections

Have you had a boss who was more technically competence than you? Did use that skill to make you better or to keep it close to the cuff?

Have you ever had a boss that's less technically competent than you? Did they hide it or were they open about it? Did they lean on you for your skill? How was that?

Which type of boss, team and environment did you prefer?

Next Steps

Always Learn

- Remember that technical competence absolutely does not matter but should not necessarily be leaned on solely. Continue to develop the skill relevant to your role, business and industry.

Encourage Other's Learning

- Give your team every ample opportunity to learn something new either through a new project, role or just simply task.

Build Learning Connections Through the Team

- Better yet, rather than you doing all the teaching, have team members who have complimentary skills and strengths team up to learn from each other.

Chapter 9

<u>Teams</u>

Not finance. Not strategy. Not technology. It is teamwork that remains the ultimate competitive advantage, both because it is so powerful and so rare.

-Pat Lencioni, author of *5 Dysfunctions of a Team*

What's the best team you've ever been on?

What did that experience feel like? What were the results of the team?

Have you been on a not so great team?

What did that feel like?

What were the results of that team?

Chances are that most of us have felt and experienced a lackluster team more often than we've experienced a great team. Why? Because real, high-performing, cohesive teams are rare.

Which is too bad because teams have the potential to unlock human and organizational potential.

Why Is Teamwork Rare?

The reason teamwork is hard work and rare is for all the same reasons marriage can be challenging. Both require a lot of vulnerability, emotional investment and pushing and growing and challenging of ourselves and being willing to do that for others.

Fun right?

No, not for most people. Definitely not for me. But I want it for myself and the teams I lead because I know, despite the discomfort involved, that when true teamwork is achieved everyone is better because of it. And that is really rewarding and fulfilling. The best things in life require a lot of work but are well worth it.

A Community at Its Core

The team relationship is unlike any other. It should be a place of trust, vulnerability, support, challenge and growth. Psychologist and marriage counselor David Schnarch calls marriage a "people development machine". And a team has the capacity to be the exact same thing, although maybe not in the same specific way.

Brené Brown, author and researcher on vulnerability and what she calls "Whole Heartedness", points out that our greatest joy and happiness in life comes from being in a safe community where we can be vulnerable. And a team, like a family, has the potential to be that for us in our work lives. Even His Holiness The Dalai Lama believes that belonging to a community is the single greatest source of happiness in life for anyone anywhere.

This is a big reason why great teamwork is hard to achieve. It requires opening up and going places with people that is healthy and required for great relationships but typically avoided at work.

Why?

Because it's uncomfortable. And some leaders think, although incorrectly, that it could lead to liability or severe negative consequences. So, the colder the better and less risky has become a norm. But with that comes less realization of fulfillment, performance and greatness.

Howard Schultz, former CEO of Starbucks, built a huge business and even industry based on our need for connection. He calls Starbucks the "third place". First, home, then work, then Starbucks, a place in between the two, a getaway and place to meet with friends, family and colleagues to connect.

In really cohesive teams, people are so personally connected and invested in each other that they want the best for each other and the entire team.

As a result, being part of a team can be one of the most rewarding experiences of our lives.

But is does require sacrifice. As Lazslo Bock puts it in his book Work Rules,

being part of a team means that on some level you've given up a level of personal freedom in exchange for accomplishing more together than you could alone.

Putting others needs above our own, especially at work, can be hard and scary. But it's in that place of vulnerability and reliance that we find connection, meaningful relationships, fulfillment, community and great achievement.

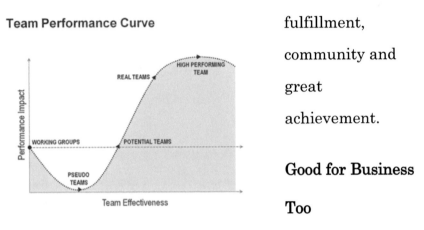

Team Performance Curve

Good for Business Too

But not only is building great teams good for people, it's also great for business. Katzenbach and Smith found that really cohesive teams can outperform non-cohesive teams and work groups of individual contributors[22]. This is why teamwork has become such a popular word in organizations. Because of the potential for great performance and results. Unfortunately, it hasn't been fully realized yet. So, both individual and organizational potential continue to be unrealized and people are disengaged in their work.

Achieving great teamwork has the potential to unlock human and organizational potential all at the same time.

A Model (or 2) for Teamwork

There are two models of teamwork that I've come across that when combined make the best framework for building the most high-performance teams that I've ever seen. They both happen to be pyramids so it worked out beautifully to just marry them together (I'm not sure of the designers of each, Pat Lencioni and Mark Miller, intended that or not). I call it the "Great Team Pyramid".

Supporting Structures of Teamwork

The first model is based on Mark Miller's outlined in his book, *The Secret of Teams*[23]. It's basically the 3 themes on the outside: Skills, Community, Talent. I call them the supporting walls of the pyramid.

Community

I don't believe Miller put these 3 elements in any particular order but I would argue that community should be at the base. Because I believe that community is the foundation for all other elements of great teams. Not necessarily more important because every element in the model is critical, but definitely where a leader should start when building or fixing a team.

I already pointed out that a team is a work community and that community can be a great source of satisfaction and fulfillment for us. But what does that look and feel like? Miller calls it, "living life together". Meaning spending time together outside of just doing the work of the team, knowing and caring about each other's passions and lives outside of work and generally caring about each other as people not just a means to an end in the workplace.

I have a friend that was a career Army officer named Brian and he puts it this way: the best teams struggle together. And he's exactly right, going through trial and tribulation in and outside of work together is all part of building that sense of community, belonging and camaraderie.

Why, How and What

Community is also where mission, values and strategy or the "Why", "How" and "What" come to life. Every community has an identity, whether stated and explicit or not.

The "Why" is the mission, purpose and reason for being. The "How" are the values, strategies, priorities

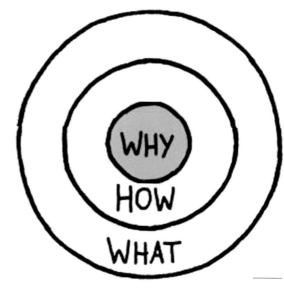

and goals. The "What" are the results and physical manifestations of the "Why" and "How" being lived out well.

I won't go into detail on each of these here since I already talked about the these before.

Just know these are very important elements to clarify and institutionalize in your team as part of building a sense of community so make sure to clarify them from the beginning and use them in guiding all decisions and actions.

Talent

Talent of course, are those natural, inherent traits we all possess that make us each unique and can be enhanced through focused training.

Having talented people on the team is vital to enable team success. Everyone knows this and it gets a lot of attention. It is rightly attributed as a leading cause of success and that's what most people, analysts and media professionals focus on in every industry, especially sports and business.

It's the responsibility of the leader, with help from the rest of the team, to systematically and thoroughly recruit and select the best and most talented people possible for the team.

Google spent twice that of other businesses in recruiting because they wanted to be like the Yankees.

Recruit (and pay) for the best and then you'll need much less infrastructure to manage and motivate them to achieve great things. Which has helped the Yankees be the highest winning team in the MLB (as much as that pains me to say

 being from the west coast).

Be Careful Although I would also argue that talent must not overshadow community. There are countless examples of teams placing far too much stake in

talent, even at the expense of their community's values and priorities. It lends to short term gains, but long-term losses.

When a team hones all other structural and behavioral elements and gets them all in sync, they can typically outperform the high talent teams. There are several inspiring examples of this: The San Antonio Spurs, the Butler Bulldogs, Seattle Seahawks and the list goes on.

When talent and community are combined is when real magic can happen. A strong community can naturally raise the talent of everyone within it.

Skills

Unlike talent, skills are more developable and tangible and technical in nature. And skill has a little more to do with the actual business of the team. In a work setting, people refer to this as "experience". Although not all experience is created equal. Experiences that also leverage our talents and push us outside our comfort zone in an intentional way lend for the best growth. The frequency and intensity of these experiences determine the quality of our "experience" and thus the level of use our talents and depth of our skills.

Behavioral Traits (or Building Blocks) of Great Teams
Now I'll talk about the center components of the pyramid. Unlike the supporting structures, these are not physical or tangible things. These are about interactions between team members.

Think of it like a garden. The 3 supporting walls are like the greenhouse, walls of the boxes, etc. **The environment**. The behaviors are like soil, water, seed, etc. **The growth material**. And then your job as the leader, to quote the great General Stanley McCrystal, is to **be the gardener**.

In other words, build and constantly monitor and nurture the environment and give the plants what they need to grow so they can do what they do best. You as the leader can't force the plants to grow. All you can do is simply provide the environment.

Like a gardener, a
leader must take
responsibility for what
he cultivates...
~Nelson Mandela

#SayQuotable

Pat Lencioni wrote the wildly popular book, *5 Dysfunctions of a Team*[24], that details the behavioral traits every team must possess to be great. Those traits are trust, conflict, commitment, accountability and results. These traits are the building blocks of the Great Team Pyramid.

Trust

Like community is to the supporting of the entire structure, trust is to every interaction and relationship within the team.

Trust is at the heart of every great team. And trust is built through vulnerability, shared experience and struggle and psychological safety. Google found in an internal study safety to be critical to their most successful teams.

1 **Psychological Safety**
Team members feel safe to take risks and be vulnerable in front of each other.

2 **Dependability**
Team members get things done on time and meet Google's high bar for excellence.

3 **Structure & Clarity**
Team members have clear roles, plans, and goals.

4 **Meaning**
Work is personally important to team members.

5 **Impact**
Team members think their work matters and creates change.

re: Work

And trust is fragile. It takes a ton of time and effort to build but only a moment to lose it. So, work tirelessly to build and maintain it. If something happens that could deteriorate trust, address it before it festers.

Conflict

This is not literally fighting, fists and all, but more about challenging of ideas and mindsets.

I love how Lencioni words this.

When teams have really high levels of trust, conflict of ideas becomes nothing more than the pursuit of truth.

This happens when the group gets together to solve a problem, make a plan or strategy or to learn and grow together as a team. In business, meetings are a team's court. The place where they come together and do the work of their team. I talked about meetings in a different post so I won't go into detail here.

Just remember that conflict is normal, healthy and necessary for a team to be successful. But it has to be built on trust and in the context of how the community norms. The style doesn't really matter as long as everyone on the team is encouraging the challenge in every direction.

Commitment

Once a team does the hard work of digging deep into a problem they know that a solution and way forward must be decided on. Because of healthy conflict, great teams know that all options have been weighed and considered so they can be confident they have a thoroughly vetted approach. This will give everyone on the team the psychological ownership over the decision being that voices were heard.

Next every team member needs to support the implementation of the approach to enable team success. They have to ensure everyone on the team is crystal clear as to what next steps are so as not to have missteps or worse a failed strategy.

Accountability

This is the hard one. Every team I've been on has struggled with this. This is the part where team members hold each other accountable for team commitments.

Why is it difficult?

The number one response? "I don't want to hurt anyone's feelings". Understandable but what happens when we don't give the feedback? The rest of the team suffers and has to work harder to produce results and the results inevitably suffer. And then the rest of team becomes resentful and trust is negatively affected.

The funny thing is most all of us want feedback from all different sources, especially our peers but everyone is scared to give it. All were doing is holding ourselves, others and our entire team back!

So, give that feedback! Do it from a trusting, trustworthy, well-intentioned place. And give it regularly and consistently so others know they can rely on you for it.

Results

Every team should have a collective goal and every member should be actively workings towards it.

Of course, every member has their own personal and professional goals but they cannot compete with or take away from the team goal in any way.

Ultimately the measure of any great team is performance. How a team and organization decide to put numbers to that is up to them and secondary to have a clear, inspiring and unifying goal.

Conclusion

This is what great teams are made of. In order for a team to be successful it must have all elements of the Great Team Pyramid. Stylistically each one will look and feel different. And that's natural, healthy and great.

I've led dozens of teams and have learned this the hard way. There were times I went very deep on the behavioral parts thinking that was enough and the team relationship was healthy but performance still wasn't there because we hadn't put structure and discipline around the supporting elements walls.

So how do you build a great team? Or many? Here are some practical approaches for you as the leader.

The truth is that teamwork is at the heart of great achievement.

John C Maxwell

Approaches to Bring the Great Team Pyramid to Life

3 Supporting Walls

1. *Community*
   - Clearly define the **"Why", "How" and "What",** plaster it all over the walls and build it into everything you do: recognition, meetings, team scorecard.
   - Have them **meet their customer** so they see the impact and importance of the team "Why" in the flesh.
   - **Live life together:** spend time together outside of work.
   - Nurture team **rituals and traditions.**

2. *Talent*
   - Thoroughly include your **team in hiring.**
   - Spend a lot of time getting to know people before you hire. Treat it almost like **courtship.**
   - **Always be looking.** As soon as you stop, you're already behind or missing out on someone great.

3. *Skills*

  o **Build in learning time** and give your team the space to do it.

  o **Have your best teach** both groups and individually.

  o **Send them off** to trainings and seminars periodically too.

4. **5 Behavioral Building Blocks**

5. *Trust*

  o **Put yourself out there first** and be vulnerable.

  o When others do the do the same, **recognize it like crazy!**

  o **Create opportunities** for people to open up to each other and/or struggle on something together.

6. *Conflict*

  o **Encourage debate**. Don't shut down emotionally charged conversations unless they're becoming personal attacks, which will be rare.

- Give ownership for problems to the team. If they feel the responsibility, they're more likely to really own the problem and outcome and thus be more willing to have healthy conflict to get a better solution.

7. *Commitment*
   - Once a decision and approach is made, **make sure everyone is absolutely clear** on what they're agreeing to.
   - Once clarity is achieved, **make sure everyone is fully on board** with the plan and has intellectually and emotionally bought in to it.

8. *Accountability*
   - DO NOT, DO NOT, **DO NOT let people complain** to you as the leader about others on the team. Your response should be, "let me know how that conversation goes". And then follow up to make sure they do it.
   - Regularly **hold group sessions** where the team can give each other feedback too. This opens the door for it in the future.

- And **you must be ultimately willing to hold everyone accountable** too. If someone is not right for the team, do the merciful thing and move them on. The rest of the team will know you're serious about accountability and respect you more for it.

9. *Results*
   - **Build your team scoreboard together** that include your "Why", "How" and "What". Part of the "What" is the thematic goal, or the most important near-term goal of the entire team.
   - Nurture your teams' personal goals and **work with them to align them with the team goals.**

Meetings

Meetings are our playing field in organizational life. Its why the god father of teamwork and organizational health and life, Pat Lencioni named his firm The Table Group.

A Meeting Approach That Works

The Table Group has a great and very thorough model for meeting structures that I personally have used for years and I stand by it wholeheartedly. I also recommend Lencioni's book on the topic, *Death By Meeting*[25]. And the model is pictured below.

Meetings Model

Meeting Type	Time required	Purpose/Format	
Daily Check-in	5 – 10 minutes	Share daily schedules and activities	• don't sit down • keep it administrative • don't cancel even when some people can't be there
Weekly Tactical	45 – 90 minutes	Review weekly activities and metrics, and resolve tactical obstacles and issues	• don't set agenda until after initial reporting • postpone strategic discussions
Monthly Strategic (or adhoc strategic)	2 – 4 hours	Discuss, analyze, brain-storm and decide upon critical issues affecting long term success	• limit to one or two topics • prepare and do research • engage in good conflict
Quarterly Off-site Review	1 – 2 days	Review strategy, competi-tive landscape, industry trends, key personnel, team development	• get out of office • focus on work; limit social activities • don't over-structure or over-burden the schedule

The 3 Cs of Meetings

My basic approach to meetings compliments the great Table Group structure. In addition to a great structure there also must be Context, Conflict and Clarity.

Context

The first thing you need to do is clarify why you are there. Is it your weekly staff meeting to help your team make decisions and solve problems to move closer to its most important near-term goal, trying to solve an important problem or for training and development purposes or setting strategy that requires team members to do homework beforehand? If you aren't sure why you are having the meeting, get clear or don't have it at all.

Conflict

Most meetings should be to make a decision or plan or strategy of some sort or provide some communication or do some training. If that's the case, then most of these meeting types require debate, discussion and that all ideas are put on the table to ensure all options are thoroughly vetted so that a decision and/or plan can be made. So, then your role as leader of the team is encourage conflict. That's right. But not arguing necessarily, but more specifically thorough and open debate of ideas. This is what makes most meetings so boring is we hold back or hold our team backs. So, seek it out, ask for opinions, let others challenge you.

Clarity

If you don't make sure to clarify what was decided on or committed to at the end of the meeting then the whole thing was a waste. Sorry, it's true. I've wasted plenty of meetings not adequately making sure everyone knew *exactly* what we should be taking away. Make sure that that is the last thing your team talks about at the end of every meeting, "what did we decide and what are we going to do after we leave this table"?

When you have great meeting structure and foundation you can transform your organization's and people's traditionally biggest pain point into one of their favorite parts of their working life.

Chapter 10

<u>Culture</u>

"I don't know how it started, either. All I know is that it's part of our corporate culture."

Culture eats strategy for breakfast.

-Peter Drucker, father of modern management theory

Most everyone has heard the above phrase. It's the mantra of the culture movement in business today.

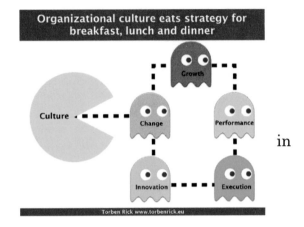

It is such a huge topic right now. Its right up there with and highly interconnected to employee engagement, innovation and disruption. I mean I'm sold! I get that it's important. I think just about everyone is convinced. The case for workplace culture has been made and made well. So many companies are working very hard to create great workplaces defined by their cultures and how employees feel within them.

Why? Because cohesive groups are better than the sum of their parts. But not all groups are created equal. There was a Harvard study done that compared similar groups that were only really different in culture, weak and toxic compared to healthy and strong. The strongest cultures outperformed the weak cultures by 765% in revenue over a 10-year period!

 The proof is in the pudding.

But what I've been wondering is, what exactly is culture, what does an effective one look like and how do you enable its creation?

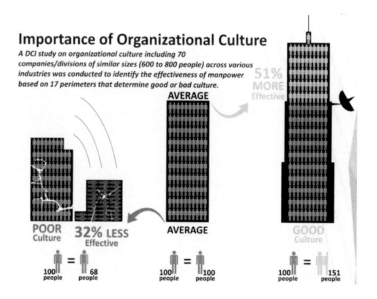

Importance of Organizational Culture

A DCI study on organizational culture including 70 companies/divisions of similar sizes (600 to 800 people) across various industries was conducted to identify the effectiveness of manpower based on 17 perimeters that determine good or bad culture.

51% MORE Effective

AVERAGE

POOR Culture **32% LESS** Effective

AVERAGE

GOOD Culture

100 people = 68 people

100 people = 100 people

100 people = 151 people

The common definition I've found so far is simply that a culture is *a collective set of mindsets, beliefs, attitudes that drive*

the actions of a group of people.

Ok, well that's pretty straightforward. But the hard part is building it intentionally and successfully.

Great ones ultimately are defined by their performance.

The good news is you make the test and the answers to the test (for the most part). Any given organization can set a lot of their own bars for success and can measure it in so many different ways. Of course, there's the common measures like revenue, profit and debt. Everyone has to make sure their finances are in order. But it definitely should not stop there.

Like I mentioned before, one company called Berry Wehmiller is an American manufacturing company that has grown to over 70 companies through acquisition. By all traditional measures it is very successful. It's leader, Bob Chapman, also wants it to be a highly conscious and human centered organization as well with a fulfilling and sought-after culture. So, to know if they are doing a great job of valuing and uplifting their employees Bob suggested they measure the divorce rate of their employees.

Incredible right!

So of course, performance is important but that comes via way of building a strong culture that people want to be a part of and can thrive in. Start with setting the bar where you want it for the basics and then add in the measurable components that more specifically showcase your culture, or what you want it to be.

A Model for Culture

Pat Lencioni designed this model and named it the Organizational Health model and it's a great roadmap for building organizational culture.

The first part is about having a **cohesive leadership team**. We talked teamwork in the last post and like so many others have pointed out that a team is a community, potentially within a larger community, and is the foundation for human and organizational greatness. So, it makes sense that Pat listed this as the first step.

Next is to **create clarity**. Clarity of purpose, goals, values, roles, norms and business function, product and/or industry or the "**Why, How and What**". All the basic and crucial stuff that you would think every organization and person within know to their core but unfortunately its rarer than you think.

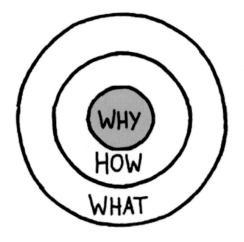

Why

I took a page out of Simon Sinek's books Start with Why and Find Your Why.

Why unites us. Why inspires us. When people have a connection through purpose, cause or belief its very powerful.

A commonality in so many writings, theories, books and approaches on team, group dynamics and culture have an element of purpose and mission.

The reason is that is where we get our energy as humans. Its built into us. We're made to have and make impact and have meaning in our lives. That meaning is different from person to person, but it's there and built into us.

Great organizations with great cultures tap into that purpose and align and nurture it like crazy to enable greatness.

How

I've mentioned the "How" several different times in Previous chapters but it is most applicable to culture. It's the foundation of culture.

Part of how is innate and not unique to a given group. Dan Coyle talks about these elements in his book the Culture Code. He found that high performing cultures had commonalities.

They are:

1. **Ensure Safety**

2. **Share Vulnerability**

3. **Build Vision**

These are the elements that Coyle found that every great culture had. So, these are crucial pillars to start with when building a culture.

Then there's the stuff that is unique to a given group. The obvious one is the purpose and vision. Nearly every team or group with have a different purpose. Therein lies some of the biggest differences needed for example in skills and talents for that particular group. And then that purpose could also dictate

Once the leadership team is cohesive and clear, then it can get down to the work of culture building which is in the **over-communicating** and **reinforcing** of the elements of clarity.

Too many leaders think their job is done once clarity is achieved, well documented, beautifully presented and shared with the organization.

That may be hard work to accomplish and noble and praise worthy, but it is not where the bulk of the work happens. There's a reason Lencioni named it *over-communicating* rather than just communicating. Because you will feel like a broken record with how many times you say, remind and share the elements of clarity. Pat calls each of the leaders in the organizations CROs or Chief Reminding Officers.

I once listened to Howard Behar, the former President of Starbucks, speak at an event at Joint Base Lewis McChord. At the end with Q&A I asked him how many times he shared the phrase "we're in the people business serving coffee" and stories that illustrated the point. His answer: over tens of thousands of times.

The point was driven home hard and I kicked myself because I had been naive as a leader in the past and got frustrated when I needed to repeat things.

But I was wrong.

Everyone needs reminding. Not because they don't care but because changing habits mindsets requires a lot of effort and reminding helps the learning curve.

The Leader

The leader sets the tone. In the Army, we called this "command climate". The unit essentially took on the temperament and values of the commander of that unit. It dawned on me most when I became a multi-unit manager. When I visited each location, even before meeting the manager, I could tell what they were like and what the valued and prioritized. It was palpable and powerful.

There is no denying that the leader is critical in culture and culture building. And I agree with Dave Marquet when he defined leadership as "decoupling the success of the organization from the personality of the leader and building greatness into the practices and people of the organization". So, in other words, the leader is vital in building, maintaining a living the values and culture AND they must build systems and people that bring it more fully to life and do not need the leader to thrive.

In every organization, culture is both what binds you together and what propels you forward – but only if you get it right.

-Vince Molinaro

Culture Building Action Steps

1. **Define your "Why" and "How".** And I recommend doing with your team, or as much of it as you can.

2. Then see your job as the leader to **recognize great culture** when you see it, **build systems** that help you reinforce it and lift it up anywhere and everywhere you can.

3. Work hard to ensure you have the **great culture foundations** too. Missions, style and feel will be different between groups, but remember the safety, vulnerable and mission are core to every great culture.

Chapter 11

Self-Development

To help others develop, start with yourself! When the boss acts like a little god and tells everyone else they need to improve, that behavior can be copied at every level of management. Every level then points out how the level below it needs to change. The end result: No one gets much better.

- Marshall Goldsmith, author and executive coach

Growing ourselves becomes so much more important when we take a position responsible for others.

If your organization offers great development opportunities, take every one of them. Fully embrace each one.

If they offer you projects and positions, take them. With each experience you will grow.

You may ask yourself, "what if I fail?" You might. Actually, you most likely will fail at some point. But in failing there's learning. Winston Churchill said that

success is simply moving from failure to failure without losing heart.

Few people would call Winston Churchill a "failure" right?

There's a process to grow. It requires us to be in tune with where we are, be clear about where we want to go and then push ourselves out of our comfort zone, practice, and keep

trying, then get feedback, reflect on the experience and try

PERSONAL DEVELOPMENT PLAN
Enter your sub headline here

Reflect on outcomes, evaluate achievements and progress. Review and re-establish future plans / goals

Self-assess skills and identify strengths and weaknesses

Review & reflect

Identify

PERSONAL DEVELOPMENT PLAN

Action & record

Plan

Develop your skills e.g. workshops, online course, seminars, self-study, conferences, mentoring, practice and more

Priorities development needs in consultation with supervisor(s) and develop a plan of action

again.

Assess

The most important thing to start with is understanding

where you are today and where you want to go.

Use every source of information at your disposal to evaluate

this. Start with yourself. Take the time to ask yourself the

follow questions:

- Where am I today?

- Am I where I want to be?
- What are my strengths as a leader?
- Where am I weak as a leader?
- What things do I like to do most in my role and on my team?
- What things do I not enjoy doing?
- What do my team, peers and boss think about me?
- What are my goals and aspirations for the future?
- How will I get there?

Once you've answered these questions and feel you have a gauge for where you stand, start to get feedback from others. Start by asking directly. And don't just ask people who like you or will just tell you all the good or only what you want to hear. Also ask people who will tell the gentle, but honest truth.

Some people won't be honest with you. Especially if you have room to grow in receiving feedback, like me. So, you will have to find another way to get feedback from everyone. 360 feedback surveys are a good way. Many companies offer them, or at the minimum you could print copies and have people fill them out anonymously if that better enables real honesty.

An important side note, if you tell your team what you are doing, that you are wanting to grow as a leader and need everyone's help, then they will give you so much respect and appreciation that chances are strong they will help you however they can.

Feedback from others is the best place to start because its real time, relatively easy to get and leadership is about people so how you affect others is the most important thing to measure.

There are other sources to leverage too like past performance reviews, team results (of course the primary ones that the organization places emphasis on are important to start with but include others too like historical employee turnover, talent sharing and promotion out of your team.

Study

There are ton of books out there on leadership, management and self-development. The way I choose books typically is based on recommendations of authors I know I already like and I look in the back of their books at their reference list to see who they've quoted or leveraged as a resource. This will give you an endless stream of already vetted books to choose from.

And you could even narrow your reading list by honing in on your specific area of developmental focus. For example, if you need to grow in coaching there are tons of great books just in that space alone but most likely fewer than leadership and management as a whole.

Personally, I like reading as much as I can, but a couple friends recently turned me on to audiobooks. One friend uses Audible and leverages his Amazon library while the other uses Overdrive and taps into the library which is the cheaper way to go and now I use both. This way I can listen to a book while driving, running, walking the dog, doing laundry, etc. Or what my Audible friend calls "windshield" time. And then if I hear something I like, I use the note app on my phone to write it down.

Podcasts are a great source of learning too and are easier to leverage. I rotate between podcasts and listening to books on my commute.

And of course, you can take formal classes too. Hopefully your organization has some internally or send people out regularly to some sort of class or seminar. If not, you can and should take the initiative to sign up for some. You may even get your organization to agree to pay for it. If all else fails, sign yourself up for one. There are lots of great options out there. And you can even go pretty cheap with online courses too on sites like Udemy.

Even cheaper is watching YouTube or Ted talks of your favorite authors. Many of them do speaking events too and hearing their messages directly may help the concepts sink it, like I know it does for me.

Unfortunately, there are not many options yet for more leadership-based programs in formal academia but more are popping up and are being increasingly offered online if you want to go a more formal, comprehensive and credentialed route.

Practice

As you learn new things about leadership and people management try them out. You can start small. If you read something relating to how to give feedback in a different way that you're doing it now, try it.

Just realize that it's going to be uncomfortable. You're not a master at the thing you're practicing yet. You may have not even had to stretch yourself in other capacities that much if you've job your job for a while. So, the feeling itself may not be as familiar.

But don't let any of these things stop you.

Make sure to allow for enough time of practice to see it you get better at the area you're trying to improve in. When we're not comfortable or its not lending to results immediately it can be easy to assume that it's not working. But don't abandon it yet. You will get an idea of when it's time to step back and reevaluate once you feel more comfortable with the tactic or strategy you're trying and based on feedback from others.

Feedback

I already pointed out the importance of feedback, so I won't rehash it. And this is more about live feedback about your growing process right now as you practice and try new things. But the same principles apply.

Feedback can and should go hand in hand with practicing, growing and trying new things.

Without feedback from people and as live as possible data, it's easy to feel lost or over or under assess what's working or not. Plus, feedback can help us adjust quickly and get better faster.

Find feedback partners with differing perspectives but with similar willingness to be thoroughly honest with you.

Reflect

Not all experience is created equal. Experience without reflection is all but wasted. I know it can be challenging to take the time to stop and think thoroughly about something that just happened or finished. Especially if the experience wasn't that fun.

But all that time you spent studying and practicing could go completely to waste if you don't think about what happened and why and what, if anything, you will take with you into the future.

I know I feel like I'm wasting time or company money when I'm not actively doing something, but once I realized that by stopping to think I'm saving myself and my team a ton of time from wasted processes or ineffective team interactions now I'm on board with "wasting time well".

So, give yourself time and space, ideally every day, especially if you're in the midst of change or practicing a new management or leadership skill.

Repeat

Now do it again. And again. And again.

Growth is a journey, a process and a messy one at that. It is not an event or destination.

Eventually you'll come to love it. We're all built to grow, develop, and become better versions of ourselves. So, once you start you won't want to stop. And don't, no matter what. You deserve it, your family and team deserve you at your best.

So good luck to you on your leadership growth journey!

LEADERSHIP DEVELOPMENT IS SELF-DEVELOPMENT.

John G Agno

Chapter 12

Organizational

Development of

Leaders

Everything rises and falls on leadership.

John C. Maxwell

"Leaders don't create followers, they create more leaders."

— Tom Peters, author and management expert

Don't Copy

Just like your third-grade teacher taught you. That's right, even though I'm showing you 8 qualities of the best people managers these are Google's. So, unless you work for Google don't copy these exactly. This is not a disclaimer out of fear of liability or something like that. It's more about respecting yourself and your organization as unique.

In other words, come up with your own variation of these people manager qualities, or at the minimum add at least one to the list that is unique to your organization, either soft or hard skill.

Or at the minimum reword some of the ones Google lists to better match your organization. For example, "Results Driver" could be "Go Getter" or "Tenacious" or "Courageous". And then you and your organizational leaders can put your own interpretation and definition on it and develop internal systems and promote, develop and cultivate based on that definition.

Leadership is the least developed and most important skill in organizations today. It's a huge problem. I've personally felt and experienced its effects in both large and small organizations. A lack of leadership and leaders in organizations holds back change, slows innovation, reduces agility, ensures low employee engagement and thus customer relationships and satisfaction with your organization.

So, unless you as an organizational leader can specifically point to what you're doing to naturally and sustainably grow leaders, chances are you may need to make it a priority.

The first thing to realize is that the way you run your organization is the single greatest factor on growing leaders within your organization.

Companies that go and find, court and hire the most talented leaders they can and then tie their hands in trying to make things better are squandering resources. It would be like buying the latest iPhone yet and keeping it the box.

As the world get smaller, faster and more complex new skills are needed.

That's why leadership is becoming so much more critical than ever before.

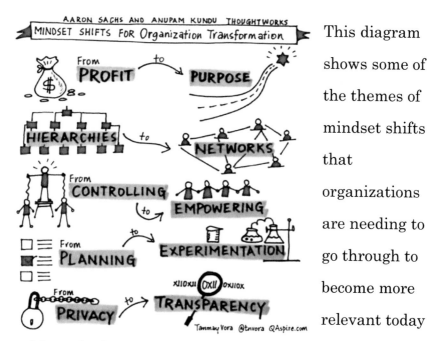

This diagram shows some of the themes of mindset shifts that organizations are needing to go through to become more relevant today and into the future. The future mindsets all require really effective leadership based on trust, cooperation and a belief that people are inherently good versus a controlling micro-management approach that looks at and uses people as a means to an end.

Safety First

Foundationally you have to make the environment **safe** first. Simon Sinek talks about this. The model he designed to illustrate his point is called the Circle of Safety. In order for people to take risks, take initiative, embrace change and trust their leaders they must feel safe.

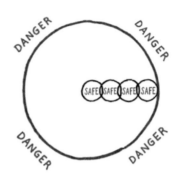

Leadership is about people. Taking care of the them. Bringing out their best. Bringing people together towards a common cause.

Leadership development is like any other training or development. In order for some to learn well and attain mastery, they have to feel safe to try, safe to take risks and safe to fail and learn from it.

Safety is critical. So, choose your words carefully, celebrate risk taking and failure for the sake of learning and growing and you will be off to the right start.

Push Down the Power

It can be scary to pass power to someone else. But you need your leaders to lead, to take initiative, advance your cause, take care of your people. That requires decision making which ultimately requires the power to make those decisions.

The best way to create active, engaged, responsible, initiative-taking leaders of the future is to give them power and responsible for decisions and outcomes as much as is possible.

Train It

Like I mentioned before leadership is about inspiring and motivating people to achieve personal and collective success and flourishing. So just teach that.

Kidding of course. There's definitely more to it than that. However, it is just that simple and that difficult.

Important people manager and leader skills include:

- **emotional intelligence**

- team leadership
- empathy and humility
- vision and goal setting
- coaching
- empowerment
- career development

Maybe you already have leaders that are great at these skills in house and the can design and teach courses based on their skill and mastery to other future leaders.

Or if you don't have that skill in house, you can always bring in a trainer or send them to targeted training.

Online courses can work for basic theoretical understanding of concepts but since leadership is about people the best training really needs to involve **people**.

Average organizations give their people something to work on. Great organizations give their people something to work toward.

-Simon Sinek

References

1. Principles. Ray Dalio. 2018.

2. Work Rules. Laszlo Bock.

3. Credibility: How Leaders Gain and Lose it, Why People Demand it. James M. Kouzes, Barry Z. Pozner. 2011.

4. One Minute Manager Meets the Monkey. Ken Blanchard.

5. The Coaching Habit. Michael Bungay Stanier.

6. Talent Code. Daniel Coyle.

7. Team of Teams. Stanley McCrystal.

8. Powerful: Building a Culture of Freedom and Responsibility. Patty McCord. 2018

9. Start With Why. Simon Sinek.

10. Turn the Ship Around. L. David Marquet.

11. Everybody Matters. Bob Chapman.

12. It's Not About the Coffee. Howard Behar.

13. How to Win Friends and Influence People. Dale Carnegie.

14. What Got You Here Won't Get You There. Marshall Goldsmith.

15. Leaders Eat Last. Simon Sinek.

16. Culture Code. Dan Coyle.

17. Organizational Health. Patrick Lencioni.

18. Politics, Solos and Turf Wars. Patrick Lencioni.

19. The Power of Habit. Charles Duhigg

20. The Profit vs. Purpose Debate… in Real Time. Korn Ferry. Kevin Cashman.
    https://www.kornferry.com/institute/profit-vs-purpose-technology

21. Conscious Capitalism. Raj Sisodia and John Mackey

22. Wisdom of Teams. John Katzenbach and Douglas Smith. 1992.

23. The Secret of Teams. Mark Miller.

24. Five Dysfunctions of a Team. Patrick Lencioni

25. Death By Meeting. Patrick Lencioni.

CCG

CCG is a leadership, teamwork, organizational culture and health training and consulting firm in the Pacific Northwest.

It's on a mission to make work better by making better people managers and leaders that build better teams and create better cultures within their organizations.

CCG offers anything and everything you need for either basic support in people manager development to full transformational consulting.

For more information please visit craigconsultinggroupccg.com.

Made in the USA
San Bernardino, CA
25 March 2019